Soul Check Motivational Quotes

Priscilla Monroe

Published by
Kingdom Kaught Publishing, LLC
Odenton, MD USA

Printed in the USA

Soul Check Motivational Quotes

ISBN 978-0-9982100-8-7

Library of Congress Control Number (LCCN):
2017944398

Soul Check Motivational Quotes

Introduction

This book is intended to help you throughout your day to day life. May you find encouragement for your soul in these short quotes.

On each page is space for you to journal a brief response on how the quote helped you change your perspective.

You have the strength to get it done

_____

_____

_____

_____

_____

_____

_____

_____

You are beautiful

_____

_____

_____

_____

_____

_____

_____

_____

You are great

_____

_____

_____

_____

_____

_____

_____

_____

_____

You are awesome

_____

_____

_____

_____

_____

_____

_____

_____

_____

Reach high for what you deserve

_____

_____

_____

_____

_____

_____

_____

_____

_____

Mind over matter

_____

_____

_____

_____

_____

_____

_____

_____

_____

Never criticize yourself

_____

_____

_____

_____

_____

_____

_____

_____

_____

Shine like a diamond

_____

_____

_____

_____

_____

_____

_____

_____

_____

I can't, isn't an option

_____

_____

_____

_____

_____

_____

_____

_____

Trust your gut

_____

_____

_____

_____

_____

_____

_____

_____

Your lips are beautiful

_____

_____

_____

_____

_____

_____

_____

_____

Dig deep

_____

_____

_____

_____

_____

_____

_____

_____

Your thighs are beautiful

_____

_____

_____

_____

_____

_____

_____

_____

_____

Your hair is lovely

_____

_____

_____

_____

_____

_____

_____

_____

_____

I love your eyes

_____

_____

_____

_____

_____

_____

_____

_____

_____

Your skin tone is gorgeous

_____

_____

_____

_____

_____

_____

_____

_____

_____

You are resilient

_____

_____

_____

_____

_____

_____

_____

_____

Your lips look soft as cotton

_____

_____

_____

_____

_____

_____

_____

_____

Your toes are perfect

_____

_____

_____

_____

_____

_____

_____

_____

_____

Quitting isn't an option

_____

_____

_____

_____

_____

_____

_____

_____

_____

You smell good

_____

_____

_____

_____

_____

_____

_____

_____

_____

Your nose was made perfectly

_____

_____

_____

_____

_____

_____

_____

_____

_____

Your eyebrows are pretty

_____

_____

_____

_____

_____

_____

_____

_____

Your ears are likeable

_____

_____

_____

_____

_____

_____

_____

_____

The shape of your mouth is stupendous

_____

_____

_____

_____

_____

_____

_____

_____

You have leadership skills

_____

_____

_____

_____

_____

_____

_____

_____

You are inspiring

_____

_____

_____

_____

_____

_____

_____

_____

_____

Be yourself

_____

_____

_____

_____

_____

_____

_____

_____

_____

Walk with a smile on your face

_____

_____

_____

_____

_____

_____

_____

_____

_____

You are relentless

_____

_____

_____

_____

_____

_____

_____

_____

_____

Keep pushing for the standards to be higher

_____

_____

_____

_____

_____

_____

_____

_____

Be unstoppable

_____

_____

_____

_____

_____

_____

_____

_____

Walk in your truth

_____

_____

_____

_____

_____

_____

_____

_____

_____

Believe

_____

_____

_____

_____

_____

_____

_____

_____

_____

Observe yourself

Smile at yourself

Laugh out loud

_____

_____

_____

_____

_____

_____

_____

_____

Giggle

_____

_____

_____

_____

_____

_____

_____

_____

Be unapologetically you

_____

_____

_____

_____

_____

_____

_____

_____

_____

Change what needs to be changed

_____

_____

_____

_____

_____

_____

_____

_____

_____

Have a tone of compassion

_____
_____
_____
_____
_____
_____
_____
_____
_____

Help someone else

_____
_____
_____
_____
_____
_____
_____
_____
_____

Know that better is better

_____

_____

_____

_____

_____

_____

_____

_____

_____

Speak highly of yourself

_____

_____

_____

_____

_____

_____

_____

_____

_____

Show-up!

_____

_____

_____

_____

_____

_____

_____

_____

Look up when you fall down, it's easier to recover

_____

_____

_____

_____

_____

_____

_____

You got this!

_____

_____

_____

_____

_____

_____

_____

_____

_____

You are fierce!

_____

_____

_____

_____

_____

_____

_____

_____

_____

Soul Check Motivational Quotes

Be moved

_____
_____
_____
_____
_____
_____
_____
_____

One step is a good start

_____
_____
_____
_____
_____
_____
_____
_____

You are a warrior

_____

_____

_____

_____

_____

_____

_____

_____

Be peaceful

_____

_____

_____

_____

_____

_____

_____

_____

Be diligent

_____

_____

_____

_____

_____

_____

_____

_____

_____

You are solid and not broken

_____

_____

_____

_____

_____

_____

_____

_____

_____

Be unmovable

_____

_____

_____

_____

_____

_____

_____

_____

_____

Choose to be strong

_____

_____

_____

_____

_____

_____

_____

_____

_____

Say it out loud, I love myself

_____

_____

_____

_____

_____

_____

_____

_____

_____

Be authentic

_____

_____

_____

_____

_____

_____

_____

_____

_____

Be graceful

_____

_____

_____

_____

_____

_____

_____

_____

_____

Turn heads for the right reasons

_____

_____

_____

_____

_____

_____

_____

_____

_____

Choose your words wisely

_____

_____

_____

_____

_____

_____

_____

_____

_____

Keep pressing on

_____

_____

_____

_____

_____

_____

_____

_____

_____

There are many directions in this journey called life

Show yourself love

Whatever isn't an option to make an excuse not to be better

_____

_____

_____

_____

_____

_____

_____

_____

Speak life

_____

_____

_____

_____

_____

_____

_____

_____

Put one foot in front of the other

Take action

Be passionate

_____

_____

_____

_____

_____

_____

_____

_____

_____

Climb over the walls

_____

_____

_____

_____

_____

_____

_____

_____

_____

Wake up with gratitude on your mind

_____

_____

_____

_____

_____

_____

_____

_____

_____

Reach for the stars

_____

_____

_____

_____

_____

_____

_____

_____

_____

Always check the twinkle in your eyes

_____

_____

_____

_____

_____

_____

_____

_____

_____

Require the best

_____

_____

_____

_____

_____

_____

_____

_____

_____

Be humble

_____

_____

_____

_____

_____

_____

_____

_____

You are innovative

_____

_____

_____

_____

_____

_____

_____

_____

Soul Check Motivational Quotes

You are amazing

_____

_____

_____

_____

_____

_____

_____

_____

_____

You are wonderful

_____

_____

_____

_____

_____

_____

_____

_____

_____

Be pleasant

_____

_____

_____

_____

_____

_____

_____

_____

You are marvelous

_____

_____

_____

_____

_____

_____

_____

_____

You are exceptional

_____

_____

_____

_____

_____

_____

_____

_____

_____

You are fantastic

_____

_____

_____

_____

_____

_____

_____

_____

_____

You are supreme

_____
_____
_____
_____
_____
_____
_____
_____
_____

You are terrific

_____
_____
_____
_____
_____
_____
_____
_____
_____

You are splendid

_____

_____

_____

_____

_____

_____

_____

_____

_____

You are enjoyable

_____

_____

_____

_____

_____

_____

_____

_____

_____

You are a blessing

_____
_____
_____
_____
_____
_____
_____
_____
_____

You are a thoughtful person

_____
_____
_____
_____
_____
_____
_____
_____
_____

You are courteous

_____
_____
_____
_____
_____
_____
_____
_____
_____

You are lovely

_____
_____
_____
_____
_____
_____
_____
_____
_____

You are likeable

You are pleasing

You are congenial

_____
_____
_____
_____
_____
_____
_____
_____
_____

You are cordial

_____
_____
_____
_____
_____
_____
_____
_____
_____

You are admirable

_____

_____

_____

_____

_____

_____

_____

_____

You are considerate

_____

_____

_____

_____

_____

_____

_____

_____

Admire yourself

_____

_____

_____

_____

_____

_____

_____

_____

Approve of yourself

_____

_____

_____

_____

_____

_____

_____

_____

You are fancy

_____

_____

_____

_____

_____

_____

_____

_____

_____

Adore yourself

_____

_____

_____

_____

_____

_____

_____

_____

_____

Treasure yourself

_____

_____

_____

_____

_____

_____

_____

_____

Marvel at yourself

_____

_____

_____

_____

_____

_____

_____

_____

Appreciate yourself

_____

_____

_____

_____

_____

_____

_____

_____

_____

You are worthy of respect

_____

_____

_____

_____

_____

_____

_____

_____

_____

Respect your time

_____

_____

_____

_____

_____

_____

_____

_____

Cherish yourself

_____

_____

_____

_____

_____

_____

_____

_____

Be fond of yourself

_____

_____

_____

_____

_____

_____

_____

_____

_____

Desire your talents

_____

_____

_____

_____

_____

_____

_____

_____

_____

Enjoy yourself

_____

_____

_____

_____

_____

_____

_____

_____

_____

Be elated

_____

_____

_____

_____

_____

_____

_____

_____

_____

Be thrilled

_____

_____

_____

_____

_____

_____

_____

_____

Be merry

_____

_____

_____

_____

_____

_____

_____

_____

You are amusing

_____

_____

_____

_____

_____

_____

_____

_____

_____

You are jovial

_____

_____

_____

_____

_____

_____

_____

_____

_____

You are dazzling

_____

_____

_____

_____

_____

_____

_____

_____

_____

You are joyful

_____

_____

_____

_____

_____

_____

_____

_____

_____

You are attractive

_____

_____

_____

_____

_____

_____

_____

_____

_____

Be victorious

_____

_____

_____

_____

_____

_____

_____

_____

_____

You are gifted

_____

_____

_____

_____

_____

_____

_____

_____

_____

You are a success

_____

_____

_____

_____

_____

_____

_____

_____

_____

You are strong

_____

_____

_____

_____

_____

_____

_____

_____

_____

You are allowed to cry

_____

_____

_____

_____

_____

_____

_____

_____

_____

You are original

_____

_____

_____

_____

_____

_____

_____

_____

You are a leader

_____

_____

_____

_____

_____

_____

_____

_____

_____

Trust your intuition

_____

_____

_____

_____

_____

_____

_____

_____

You are intelligent

_____

_____

_____

_____

_____

_____

_____

_____

You have everything it takes

_____

_____

_____

_____

_____

_____

_____

_____

You are brave

_____

_____

_____

_____

_____

_____

_____

_____

Learn to be free

_____

_____

_____

_____

_____

_____

_____

_____

_____

Keep a positive attitude

_____

_____

_____

_____

_____

_____

_____

_____

_____

You are worth pampering yourself

_____

_____

_____

_____

_____

_____

_____

_____

_____

Celebrate your progress, you are worthy

_____

_____

_____

_____

_____

_____

_____

_____

_____

You are adventurous

_____

_____

_____

_____

_____

_____

_____

_____

_____

It's ok to be cool

_____

_____

_____

_____

_____

_____

_____

_____

_____

Talk, someone wants to hear you

_____

_____

_____

_____

_____

_____

_____

_____

You are enough

_____

_____

_____

_____

_____

_____

_____

_____

Your story is vital

_____

_____

_____

_____

_____

_____

_____

_____

_____

Dance yourself a new dance

_____

_____

_____

_____

_____

_____

_____

_____

_____

Soul Check Motivational Quotes

You are teachable

_____
_____
_____
_____
_____
_____
_____
_____
_____

The details about you make you unique

_____
_____
_____
_____
_____
_____
_____
_____
_____

Step your game up, you got this!

_____

_____

_____

_____

_____

_____

_____

_____

_____

Being a mystery is ok

_____

_____

_____

_____

_____

_____

_____

_____

_____

You are a trendsetter

_____

_____

_____

_____

_____

_____

_____

_____

_____

Overpower the small negative voice

_____

_____

_____

_____

_____

_____

_____

_____

_____

Be independent

_____
_____
_____
_____
_____
_____
_____
_____
_____

Someone wants to be your friend

_____
_____
_____
_____
_____
_____
_____
_____
_____

Your wisdom is powerful

_____

_____

_____

_____

_____

_____

_____

_____

It's ok to move on

_____

_____

_____

_____

_____

_____

_____

_____

A do over is ok

_____
_____
_____
_____
_____
_____
_____
_____
_____

You are worth the process

_____
_____
_____
_____
_____
_____
_____
_____
_____

Press on

_____

_____

_____

_____

_____

_____

_____

_____

_____

Soul Check Ministries' purpose is to mentor and train people in entrepreneurial development and to build character and confidence in the lives of young people.

This book is being used as a tool to empower and raise self-esteem to help lower suicide in our Nation.

CPSIA information can be obtained
at www.ICGtesting.com
Printed in the USA
BVHW04s0344040918
526125BV00005B/39/P